VICTORY
OVER
PORN

VICTORY OVER PORN

Escape Your Guilt and Shame

DARRIN ELFORD

DARRIN ELFORD
PREMIUM BOOKS

About the Author

For years, the author struggled in the grip of porn addiction. What started as a way to escape stress and numb painful emotions slowly turned into a chain that shackled his life. In the darkest moments, he felt trapped in a cycle of shame, guilt, and isolation, with each relapse pushing him deeper into despair. Porn wasn't just a habit - it was consuming his time, destroying his relationships, and his self-respect with two failed marriage as proof of its devastating effects.

But through relentless self-reflection, painful honesty, and a determination to break free, he found a way out. Step by step, he reclaimed my life and won the battle. It wasn't easy, and it wasn't immediate, but over time, he began to rebuild the man I was meant to be. Today, he lives a life free from the addiction that once held him captive. He has found purpose, joy, and connection again, and is now passionate about helping others do the same.

This book is his story - a raw, real, and authentic account of overcoming the darkness of porn addiction. Through his journey, he discovered not just freedom from porn, but a life of true fulfilment. He is proof, that, no matter how deep the darkness, there is always a way out.

This book has taken real vulnerability, is raw and authentic about his personal journey and ultimate victory over porn and masturbation.

What's more exciting is that victory over porn can be your birth right by reading this book and undertaking the practical steps outlined in the chapters. Welcome to a porn-free life and to escaping the guilt and shame you feel.

Acknowledgements

First and foremost, I want to thank you for picking up this book and deciding to make a change in your life. It takes courage to confront an addiction, and by opening these pages, you've already taken the first step toward freedom.

I would like to express my deep gratitude to the men who have shared their personal stories with me over the years. Your vulnerability, strength, and honesty have been an inspiration. You have helped me understand the true pain of addiction, but more importantly, you've shown me the power of transformation. Your journeys are the foundation of this book.

To my family and friends, thank you for your unwavering support. Your belief in me, even when I struggled, has been a constant reminder that change is possible. I could not have written this book without your love and encouragement.

To the many professionals - therapists, coaches, and mentors - who guided me through my own journey, thank you. Your expertise and compassion helped me understand that overcoming addiction is not just about willpower, but about healing, self-awareness, and building new habits.

Finally, to my fellow "quitters," you are my true heroes. I see your struggle, and I understand the battle. I honor your commitment to change. You are not alone, and together, we are stronger.

This book is dedicated to you - the man who is ready to break free, to reclaim his life, and to step into the life he was always meant to live. I believe in you, and I'm proud to walk this path with you.

Table of Contents

Introduction

If you're holding this book, it means you've come to a turning point in your life. Maybe you're tired of feeling trapped by the grip of porn and masturbation. Perhaps you've tried to quit before, only to fall back into the same habits. Or maybe, you've reached a point where the pain of continuing this cycle has become too much to ignore. Whatever your reason for picking up this book, I want you to know that you are not alone, and most importantly, **change is possible**.

I know because I've been where you are. I've been caught in the cycle of shame, frustration, and helplessness. For years, porn and masturbation held control over my life, affecting my relationships, my self-esteem, and my future. I felt disconnected, lost, and powerless to stop. But I made a choice—a choice to break free. And I want to help you do the same.

This book is not about shame or judgment. It's about reclaiming your life. The journey ahead may seem difficult, but it is one worth taking. In these pages, you will find a clear, step-by-step plan to help you quit porn and masturbation for good. You will learn practical tools to manage cravings, rebuild your self-esteem, and transform your life.

But this isn't just about stopping a habit. It's about rebuilding your life from the ground up - restoring your confidence, your relationships, and your sense of purpose. It's about becoming the man you were always meant to be, living a life full of freedom, focus, and fulfilment.

I'm here to guide you through every stage of the process, with simple, actionable steps and the wisdom I've gained from my own journey and the stories of countless others who have successfully overcome this addiction. Along the way, you'll discover that quitting porn isn't just about eliminating something harmful—it's about creating a space for something much greater.

If you're ready to take control of your life and break free from the chains of addiction, this book will show you how. It won't be easy, but it will be worth it. You have the strength inside you to overcome this, and I'm here to help you every step of the way. Let's get started.

1

The Darkness of Porn Addiction

Defining Porn Addiction and Its Impact

Porn addiction isn't something we often talk about openly, but if you're reading this, chances are it has been controlling your life in ways you might not fully understand. Porn addiction is when someone consistently watches pornography despite negative consequences, feeling unable to stop, even when they want to. It's a cycle that becomes more powerful over time. The brain gets conditioned to crave the intense stimulation that porn provides, leading to a compulsion that can feel impossible to break.

This addiction isn't just about watching something on a screen. It affects every part of your life—your mind, your emotions, and even your body.

- **Mental Health**

The more you watch porn, the more your brain gets used to the constant flood of dopamine—the chemical that gives you feelings of pleasure and reward. Over time, your brain needs more intense material to get the same feeling, which can lead to a desensitization effect. This makes it harder to enjoy normal life experiences. Activities like spending time with family or focusing on work start to feel less satisfying because your brain is accustomed to the extreme highs of pornography. This can lead to feelings of depression, anxiety, and a lack of motivation.

- **Emotional Health**

Porn can create emotional numbness. As you rely more on porn to escape stress, boredom, or negative emotions, you start to disconnect from your true feelings. This can leave you feeling empty, lost, or detached from your own emotional life. You might feel like something is missing, but you don't know what it is.

- **Physical Health**

Porn addiction can affect your body in ways you might not realize. There's a phenomenon called "porn-induced erectile dysfunction" (PIED) where men who regularly watch porn struggle with performance in real-life sexual situations. This happens because your brain becomes wired to respond to pornographic images, making it hard to become aroused in the presence of a real person. Additionally, the act of frequent masturbation can lead to physical exhaustion, affecting your energy and focus throughout the day.

How Porn Addiction Affects Your Life

Porn doesn't exist in a vacuum. Its impact reaches far beyond just the time you spend watching videos. The more you allow this addiction to control you, the more it eats away at other important aspects of your life:

- **Relationships**

Porn can create distance in your relationships, especially with a partner. When you're consumed by an addiction, intimacy with others starts to feel less fulfilling. You may find yourself less emotionally present or unable to connect in meaningful ways. In some cases, it may lead to broken relationships due to trust issues or the inability to communicate openly about your needs. It can also foster unrealistic expectations about sex and intimacy, making it harder to truly connect with another person.

- **Productivity and Focus**

If you're spending hours watching porn, that's hours you're not spending on things that matter. Whether it's work, hobbies, or goals, porn steals your focus and energy. It becomes a distraction that makes you less productive, and as your performance slips, your confidence takes a hit. Over time, this can create a sense of hopelessness or dissatisfaction in your professional life.

- **Self-Esteem**

When you're addicted to porn, your self-worth is often tied to a cycle of shame and secrecy. You may feel disgusted with yourself for not being able to control your urges, which can lead to feelings of inadequacy. Over time, this erodes your self-esteem and confidence, making it even harder to break free from the addiction. You might compare yourself to others, feeling like you're the only one struggling, which deepens the sense of isolation.

- **Life Satisfaction**

Ultimately, porn addiction can make life feel hollow. It takes away from real, fulfilling experiences, replacing them with short-term gratification that never satisfies. You may notice that, despite spending hours indulging in your addiction, you feel emptier than before. This emptiness makes everything else in life—work, relationships, and hobbies—feel less meaningful.

Real-Life Stories of Men Struggling with Porn Addiction

Let me share a few stories to make this more real for you. These are men who've been where you are now, who've struggled, but ultimately found the strength to reclaim their lives.

John's Story

John was in his late twenties when he realized that porn had taken over his life. At first, it was just something he did occasionally to relieve stress. But over time, he found himself watching for hours, every day. His work performance suffered because he couldn't focus. He avoided socializing, feeling embarrassed about the life he was living. His relationship with his girlfriend was on the brink of collapse because he felt distant and disconnected. But the turning point came when he started noticing his physical health deteriorating. He could no longer get aroused in real-life situations. That was the moment he realized that porn was no longer just a habit—it was an addiction. And it was ruining his life.

John didn't quit overnight. It took time, effort, and patience. But eventually, through therapy, accountability, and consistent work, he started to feel alive again. He reconnected with his girlfriend, and his work performance improved. John found the courage to share his story, knowing that his journey could help others.

Mark's Story

Mark had been watching porn since he was 13 years old. Over the years, it became a secret escape, something that numbed him from the pressures of life. But by his mid-thirties, Mark's addiction had taken a toll on his marriage. His wife suspected something was wrong, but Mark couldn't bring himself to tell her the truth. He was embarrassed. His sex life was non-existent, and he felt emotionally distant from her. He felt trapped. It wasn't until he hit rock bottom—feeling disconnected from his own family and unsure of who he had become—that he realized he needed to change.

Mark sought help and worked with a therapist who specialized in porn addiction. Through that process, he was able to rebuild his relationship with his wife and his own sense of self-worth. He learned that it wasn't just about stopping the behavior - it was about healing emotionally, physically, and mentally. Now, Mark is living a much more connected and fulfilling life.

The Shame and Isolation of Porn Addiction

One of the hardest parts of porn addiction is the shame that often accompanies it. You might feel like you're the only one who is struggling. It's easy to feel isolated, as if no one else understands what you're going through. But here's the truth: You are not alone.

Porn thrives in secrecy. It encourages isolation, making you believe that your addiction is something you need to hide from the world. The more you keep it to yourself, the more powerful the shame becomes. You start feeling like you're broken, like there's no way out. But the moment you begin to confront this addiction openly, whether it's with a therapist, a support group, or someone you trust, the power it holds over you starts to fade.

Hope and Transformation: Change Is Possible

I want you to understand something very important: **change is possible**. I've lived through the darkness of addiction, and I can tell you from experience that freedom is achievable. It won't be easy, and it won't happen overnight, but you have the strength inside you to reclaim your life.

This book is not just about quitting porn—it's about transforming your life. It's about healing your mind, body, and emotions. It's about rebuilding relationships, restoring your self-esteem, and finding a life of purpose. There is hope, and you can create the life you deserve.

The first step is acknowledging where you are. The next step is deciding that you want something better. And the journey that follows will be one of the most rewarding steps you ever take. Let's begin.

My Personal Darkness from Porn Addiction

The darkness I experienced because of my porn addiction wasn't something that could be easily seen on the surface. It wasn't always about the shame I felt when I relapsed or the guilt that weighed on me. It was deeper than that. The reality of living with this addiction was a slow, suffocating feeling that I couldn't escape.

I remember the nights when the urge would hit me like a wave—constant, overwhelming, and impossible to ignore. I felt trapped. Every time I gave in, I told myself it would be the last time. But it never was. The promise I made to myself became meaningless. I would act on the urge, and once the immediate pleasure faded, it was like a deep void opened up. That void wasn't filled with satisfaction; it was filled with **emptiness**. Every time I fed the addiction, I felt more hollow. Porn was meant to be a quick escape from stress, from loneliness, from everything that felt out of control. But it never gave me what I truly needed.

I was hiding. I was hiding from myself. From my pain. From the things I didn't want to face. And with each relapse, the darkness grew. It was like living with a secret that consumed me. I couldn't tell anyone about it. I felt **isolated**—completely alone in my struggle. The shame was overwhelming. And the worst part? The guilt would come rushing in, making me feel like I was someone I didn't want to be. The man I was becoming wasn't someone I recognized. I felt like I was trapped in a cycle of self-destruction. Porn had become my crutch, my escape, but it was also the very thing that kept me stuck.

But the emotional darkness was not just in the moments of acting on the addiction. It was in the aftermath. The hours I wasted, the time I would never get back. I realized how much **life** was slipping through my fingers. Every hour spent in front of a screen was an hour lost. I felt disconnected from the world. My relationships were strained. I wasn't the person I wanted to be for my family or my friends. I wasn't showing up as the partner I needed to be. And every time I disappointed them, it added to the growing weight of my guilt.

There was a moment I'll never forget—the moment I saw the full extent of the damage. I had just relapsed, again. I sat there, looking at myself in the mirror, and I didn't recognize the person looking back. I was exhausted. I was **broken.** My self-esteem was crushed, and I couldn't even look at myself with any sort of respect. I had betrayed myself again.

Porn was no longer just a habit; it had become a force that controlled my thoughts, my actions, and my entire life. It was like I was trapped in a cage of my own making. I was a prisoner to my addiction. And the hardest part was realizing that no one else could free me. Only I could do that. But in that moment of darkness, I didn't even believe I could.

That's when I hit my breaking point. When I was consumed by shame, by regret, and by hopelessness. It felt like my life was slipping away, and I had nothing left to give. But even in the deepest darkness, I started to realize something: I could choose to break free. I didn't have to remain stuck. The addiction had become my identity, but it didn't have to define me forever.

I don't want you to feel sorry for me. I'm sharing this to show you how deep the darkness can go, and why it's so important to face it. I was living in the shadows for so long, and I know how hard it is to imagine a way out. But if you're in that darkness right now, I need you to know that it doesn't have to be this way. The journey ahead won't be easy, but **it is possible** to find light again. And the first step begins with you.

For me, that first step was acknowledging that I was more than the addiction. It was realizing that there was a life waiting for me, a life without the chains of porn holding me back. And once I made that decision, I started to move toward that freedom. It wasn't an overnight change, but it was a change. One decision at a time.

So, if you're reading this and you feel like you're in that same dark place, know that **you're not alone**. I've been there, and I made it out. You can too. It's not easy, but it is worth it. The first step is to realize that there's a way forward—through the darkness, into the light.

Action: Recognize your Porn Addiction

Before you can break free from something, you first have to fully understand its grip on your life. This isn't about feeling bad about yourself or sinking deeper into shame. It's about being honest with where you are right now. The first step to reclaiming your life is recognizing how porn and masturbation have affected you and the areas of your life that have suffered because of it.

Take a moment to reflect on how often you turn to porn, how long you've been using it, and what you've allowed it to take away from you. Maybe it's your focus at work or your energy to engage in real relationships. Perhaps it's your ability to experience joy in everyday things, or the peace of mind you once had but lost along the way.

Porn isn't just an isolated habit. It's an addiction that can seep into every corner of your life. It's something that, over time, can erode your self-esteem, damage your relationships, and leave you feeling trapped in a cycle of shame and secrecy. It might have started as a casual escape, a way to pass time or cope with stress. But now, it has become a powerful force, one that makes you feel powerless.

In this chapter, I want you to acknowledge the ways in which porn and masturbation have been controlling you. Ask yourself: **How has this addiction affected my mental and emotional well-being? How has it affected my relationships? My goals? My self-worth?** It might be uncomfortable to think about, but this is a crucial part of the process.

It's important to face the reality of how deeply this addiction has rooted itself in your life. And while that might seem overwhelming at first, it's also empowering. **The moment you truly see the impact this addiction has on you is the moment you can begin to take control again.**

Acknowledging the hold that porn and masturbation have on your life doesn't mean you're stuck. It means you're ready to make a change. It's the first step in the journey toward freedom. And once you recognize where you are, you'll be ready to take the next steps toward where you want to be.

This isn't about perfection. It's about progress. By recognizing the reality of the situation, you're giving yourself the clarity you need to move forward. You're starting the journey of reclaiming your life—and that journey begins with you, right here, right now.

2

Your Need to Quit Porn

Hidden Costs of Porn Addiction

When we think about the consequences of porn use, it's easy to focus on the immediate effects: the time spent watching, the physical acts, or the feeling of shame afterward. But the true cost of porn addiction goes much deeper. The mental and emotional toll it takes on a person can last far beyond the screen. If you're struggling with this addiction, you've likely felt some of these effects yourself, even if they're hard to admit. And it's not just about the obvious problems—it's the invisible ones that hurt the most.

One of the biggest emotional consequences of continued porn use is **numbness**. Over time, watching porn and masturbating can dull your ability to connect with your emotions. You might feel emotionally distant from people around you, even those you care about. You stop experiencing the same joy or satisfaction in life because your brain is constantly chasing the next high, the next rush of dopamine. The world outside of the screen starts to feel less exciting, less meaningful. You may even start to believe that your relationships, your work, or your dreams just aren't as fulfilling as they should be.

Then there's the **mental exhaustion**. The constant need to escape into porn takes a toll on your focus and your ability to think clearly. You might find yourself distracted, unable to focus on your goals or responsibilities. Your productivity suffers, and you might feel like you're drifting through life without direction. Every time you give in to the urge to watch, you weaken your ability to focus on the things that truly matter.

This cycle of escape and distraction keeps you trapped in a loop that's hard to break.

Porn also affects your **self-esteem**. The shame that comes with it can be crushing. You may feel like you're not living up to your potential, that you're weak for not being able to quit. The longer the addiction continues, the worse you feel about yourself. It can lead to feelings of guilt, hopelessness, and even self-loathing. You might compare yourself to others who seem to have their lives together, all while feeling like you're falling short. This is a dangerous place to be, because it makes the idea of change feel impossible.

Reflecting on Your Life: The Lost Time, Missed Opportunities, and Fractured Relationships

When I look back on my own journey with porn, one of the things that hit me hardest was the **lost time**. Time I could've spent growing, building relationships, or chasing my dreams. Instead, I spent hours in isolation, feeding an addiction that was stealing my life away. It wasn't just the hours I wasted watching porn—it was the time I didn't spend with my friends, my family, or on things that mattered to me. I missed out on opportunities to grow as a person and develop the skills that would help me achieve my goals.

Think about your own life. How much time have you lost to this addiction? How many moments did you let slip by while you were caught up in a cycle of shame and escape? Every hour spent in front of a screen is an hour you could have used to build the life you truly want. It's hard to count the opportunities you've missed, the dreams you've pushed aside, and the potential you've left untapped.

And what about your relationships? If you're like many men who struggle with this addiction, porn has created distance between you and the people you care about. Maybe it's your partner, who you've pushed away because you've been emotionally unavailable or disconnected.

Maybe it's your friends, who you've neglected because you've preferred to hide away in the comfort of your addiction. Porn feeds **isolation**. It convinces you that the only real connection you need is with a screen, and it convinces you that you don't need anyone else. But that's a lie. The truth is, real connection is one of the most important things we have in life—and porn robs you of that.

As you reflect on your life, it's important to think about these lost moments. The time, opportunities, and relationships that have been affected by your addiction. This reflection isn't meant to make you feel guilty—it's meant to help you **wake up** to the reality of what's happening. You deserve more than this. You deserve a life full of meaning, connection, and purpose.

The Breaking Point – The Moment of Clarity

At some point, most men who struggle with porn addiction experience a **breaking point**. This is the moment when the pain of continuing on the same path becomes unbearable. For some, it's the realization that they're losing their partner, their career, or their sense of self-worth. For others, it's the moment when they look in the mirror and see someone they don't recognize. That was the moment for me.

I had to face the reality that if I didn't make a change, I was going to lose everything that mattered. I didn't want to be the guy who looked back on his life with regret, wondering what could have been. I didn't want to be a slave to my addiction anymore.

This moment of clarity is different for everyone, but it's always a wake-up call. It's when you finally admit to yourself that you're stuck, and you can't keep going down this path without losing more of what you love.

It's painful to realize how far you've fallen, but it's also **empowering**. It's the moment you decide that enough is enough. It's the moment you say, "I won't let this control me anymore. I won't let this take any more from me."

The Power of Decision-Making – Taking the First Step

This is where the power of **decision-making** comes in. Making the decision to quit is the first and most important step toward lasting change. It's not about being perfect—it's about choosing to take control of your life. When you make a firm decision, you're telling yourself that you are worth more than this addiction. You're choosing the future over the past.

Your decision to quit porn is the foundation of everything that follows. Without that decision, nothing will change. But with it, you create the space for transformation. Every journey begins with a single step, and that step is your **decision** to change.

Building a Strong "Why" – Your Motivation for Quitting

But deciding to quit is only the beginning. To truly make lasting change, you need to have a strong **"why"**—a deeper motivation that will keep you going when things get tough. Your "why" is the reason you're choosing to quit porn in the first place. It's the fuel that will drive you through the difficult moments and keep you focused on your goal.

For some, the "why" is **family**. You might be tired of the way your addiction has affected your relationship with your partner or children. You want to be present, emotionally available, and connected to them. You want to build a healthy, loving relationship, and you know that quitting porn is the key to making that happen.

For others, it might be about **self-respect**. You're tired of the guilt and shame that comes with this addiction. You want to feel good about yourself again. You want to restore your confidence and live with integrity.

Maybe your "why" is about **spiritual growth**. If your faith or personal beliefs are important to you, quitting porn might be about reconnecting with your higher self or your values. It's about living a life that aligns with who you truly are, not the person the addiction has turned you into.

Whatever your "why" is, it must be **strong** and **personal**. Your "why" will give you the strength to keep going when the road gets tough. It will remind you why it's all worth it.

Conclusion: The Journey Begins with You

The decision to quit porn isn't just about stopping a habit—it's about taking back control of your life. It's about making the choice to invest in a better future for yourself, your relationships, and your well-being. You have the power to change. The question is, are you ready to take the first step? The journey starts now.

My Personal Motivation to Quit Porn

There was a time when porn felt like my escape. It wasn't about sex or pleasure—it was about **numbing** the pain, the stress, and the emptiness I felt inside. But the more I used it, the deeper I sank into the darkness. What I thought was an escape only pulled me further into a world of isolation, guilt, and shame. I was living a lie, and the hardest part was that I couldn't see a way out.

But something inside me knew I had to change. I couldn't continue down this path. The reality of my life started to sink in, and it was painful. I looked around at the wreckage—the relationships I had neglected, the time I had wasted, the opportunities I had missed—and I realized that I was losing myself. I was losing the man I wanted to be.

The truth hit me like a punch to the gut: **porn was stealing my life**. It wasn't just about the immediate relief it gave me. It was about the long-term consequences. I wasn't present with the people I loved. I wasn't showing up for myself or my future. The more I turned to porn, the further I drifted from my goals, my values, and the life I wanted to build. Every time I relapsed, I felt like I was betraying not just my relationships, but my **own sense of self-respect**.

But that wasn't the worst part. The worst part was the emotional wreckage I was causing. I was ashamed of myself, and I couldn't even look in the mirror. I was spiraling, but I didn't know how to stop. I felt **empty** and **lost**, and I didn't know where to turn. I couldn't keep living like that, pretending everything was okay when deep down, I knew it wasn't.

I had to find a reason to quit. A reason so strong that I couldn't ignore it. It couldn't just be about the surface-level issues. It had to come from a place of deep, **heartfelt motivation**.

For me, that reason came from realizing how much I was hurting the people around me—especially the ones who loved me the most. I saw the toll it was taking on my relationships. My partner deserved more than a man who was emotionally distant and distracted. My friends deserved someone who would show up for them, not someone who was checked out because he was caught up in his addiction. And, most importantly, **I deserved better** than to live a life shackled by porn.

But even more than that, I realized something crucial: **I had a purpose**. Deep down, I knew I wasn't meant to live this way. I wasn't meant to be a slave to a screen. I wasn't meant to waste my life chasing temporary pleasure at the expense of real, lasting fulfillment. I had dreams, ambitions, and a future that I was throwing away. I was **worth** more than the dark, empty place porn had trapped me in.

That was my turning point. I couldn't let porn define me anymore. I couldn't let it keep me from becoming the man I was supposed to be. The man who is present for his family, who works toward his goals with integrity, who loves himself enough to break free from what holds him back.

It wasn't easy. And it wasn't immediate. But every day, I woke up with the realization that **I could change**. I could rewrite my story. It would take time, effort, and a lot of painful honesty with myself, but I was willing to do it. I had to do it—for my future, for my relationships, and for the man I wanted to be.

I remember feeling overwhelmed by how much I had to heal. The shame, the guilt, the self-loathing—I had to work through all of it. But I kept reminding myself: **this wasn't the end. It was just the beginning**. I had to make the decision to face the darkness, to look it straight in the eye, and to say, "I'm done. I'm ready to be free."

It's easy to feel hopeless when you're caught in the cycle of addiction. But if you're reading this and you feel like you're stuck, I want you to know something: **you can break free**. I did. And if I can, so can you.

The reason to quit porn has to come from a place of deep understanding of what it's costing you. It's not just about avoiding shame—it's about realizing what you're losing. Your time. Your connections. Your potential. And most importantly, your peace of mind.

When I finally made the decision to quit, I didn't just stop watching porn. I started **reclaiming my life**. I began to rebuild the relationships I'd neglected. I started to focus on things that brought me joy, fulfilment, and real connection. I worked on my self-worth and stopped letting my addiction dictate who I was. I discovered that my freedom was not just about quitting porn—it was about **embracing the life I was meant to live**.

It's hard. It's painful. But I promise you, the freedom on the other side is worth it. You can reclaim your life. You can heal the wounds. And you can rebuild a future that's better than you ever imagined. But it starts with a choice: to look at the reality of your addiction and say, "I'm ready to quit." And then, every single day, take steps toward making that choice a reality.

Action: Assess Your Need to Quit Porn

When I was deep in my addiction, I didn't think much about the future. I told myself that I could quit anytime, that it wasn't a big deal. But as time passed, I began to realize something important: **the longer I waited to make a real commitment to change, the worse things were going to get.**

I'll be honest, for a long time, I wasn't ready to commit to quitting. I'd start and stop, tell myself I'd quit for good, and then slip back into old habits. But that cycle kept me stuck, and it wasn't until I truly understood the urgency of making a change that I began to see real progress. Porn was stealing more than just my time—it was stealing my life.

You might be feeling the same way right now. Maybe you've tried quitting before and failed. Maybe you've told yourself that you'll do it tomorrow, or next week. But here's the thing: **If you don't commit to quitting porn right now, nothing will change.** The problem is real, and it's only getting worse. This isn't something you can keep putting off. If you don't make the commitment today, you'll continue down a path that leads to more pain, more lost time, and more missed opportunities.

Understanding the urgency of quitting is the first step toward taking action. It's time to stop waiting for the "perfect moment" and face the reality of your situation. Change isn't easy, but it is possible. And the sooner you make the commitment, the sooner you can begin to rebuild your life.

The Power of Commitment

Committing to quit isn't just about stopping a bad habit—it's about choosing to live a better life. It's about deciding to take control, to make a stand for your health, your relationships, and your future. When you commit, you're saying that you value yourself and your well-being more than the fleeting pleasure that porn provides.

I want you to imagine what life will look like once you've broken free. Picture yourself free from the shame, the isolation, the guilt. Think about how good it will feel to no longer be controlled by something that has no real value. That vision of a better life is what will drive you forward. Your commitment to quit becomes your foundation—the solid ground on which everything else is built.

Why You Want to Quit – Write It Down

To make a strong commitment, it's important to have a **clear reason** for why you're doing this. Without a solid "why," it's easy to lose motivation when things get tough. So, I want you to take a moment and **write down your reasons** for quitting porn. Be honest with yourself, and dig deep. Think about how this addiction has affected your life and what you stand to gain by quitting.

Here are some common reasons men decide to quit:

- **Restoring Relationships:**

Porn can put a strain on your relationships with your partner, friends, and family. You might feel emotionally distant or disconnected from the people you care about. By quitting, you can start to rebuild trust and reconnect on a deeper level.

- **Improving Self-Esteem:**

Porn can leave you feeling ashamed and unworthy. It can erode your confidence and make you believe you're less than you are. Quitting porn can help restore your self-respect and allow you to see yourself as someone capable of change and growth.

- **Reclaiming Time and Focus:**

Every hour spent on porn is time you could be using for something more meaningful. Whether it's your career, hobbies, or personal goals, quitting porn gives you the freedom to focus on the things that matter most to you.

- **Physical and Mental Health:**

Porn addiction has been linked to issues like erectile dysfunction, depression, and anxiety. Quitting porn can help improve your mental and physical health, allowing you to feel more energized, focused, and emotionally balanced.

- **Living a Life of Integrity:**

If you've been lying to yourself or others about your porn use, quitting can help you align your actions with your values. It's about living with honesty and integrity, free from the secrets that weigh you down.

Write down **five reasons why you want to quit porn**. Keep these reasons somewhere visible so that when the going gets tough, you have reminders of what you're fighting for.

Assessing the Impacts of Porn on Your Life

Now that you've written down why you want to quit, it's time to think about the **real impacts** porn has had on your life. Take a moment to reflect on how this addiction has affected your mental, emotional, and physical well-being. Ask yourself these questions:

- **How has porn affected my relationships?**

Have I pushed people away? Have I struggled to connect with my partner or friends? Has porn caused trust issues or emotional distance?

- **What impact has porn had on my work or productivity?**

Am I distracted? Have I lost focus? Have I missed opportunities because I've been too consumed by the addiction?

- **How has porn impacted my self-worth?**

Do I feel guilty or ashamed? Have I lost confidence in myself? Do I feel like I'm not living up to my potential?

- **How has porn affected my physical health?**

Have I experienced any problems, like erectile dysfunction or low energy? How has this affected my overall well-being?

Write down your answers to these questions. Be honest with yourself. This will help you see the full extent of the damage caused by porn. It may be difficult to face, but **acknowledging the impact** is the first step in creating real change.

Developing Strategies for Success

Now that you've made the commitment to quit and identified why you want to quit, it's time to develop a plan to succeed. Quitting porn isn't easy, but with the right strategies, you can break free. Here are some practical steps to help you succeed:

1. **Set Clear, Measurable Goals:**

   Instead of focusing on quitting forever, set smaller, measurable goals. For example, you might aim to go one day, one week, or one month without porn. Celebrate each milestone along the way to keep yourself motivated.

2. **Create Accountability:**

   Share your commitment with someone you trust—a friend, a partner, or a therapist. Accountability can help keep you on track and provide support when you feel tempted to relapse.

3. **Identify Triggers:**

   Think about the situations, feelings, or thoughts that lead you to watch porn. Is it stress? Loneliness? Boredom? Once you identify your triggers, you can work on finding healthier ways to cope with them.

4. **Find Healthy Alternatives:**

   Replace the time spent on porn with healthier habits. Start exercising, pick up a new hobby, or spend time with friends and family. Engaging in activities that bring you joy and fulfilment will help fill the void left by porn.

5. **Practice Self-Compassion:**

   There will be times when you slip up. When this happens, don't beat yourself up. It's important to practice self-compassion and remember that recovery is a journey, not a destination. Learn from your mistakes, get back on track, and keep moving forward.

6. **Visualize Your Success:**

   Spend time each day visualizing what your life will look like once you've quit. Picture yourself more confident, connected, and fulfilled. Hold onto that vision as a reminder of why you're doing this.

Conclusion: Your Commitment is the First Step

You've taken the first step in making a real commitment to quit. It won't be easy, but it will be worth it. The strategies you've developed, along with the reasons you've identified, will help guide you on your journey.

Remember, the urgency of change is real. If you continue down the path of addiction, you risk losing more of what matters most. But by committing today, you're taking control of your life. You're choosing a future of health, happiness, and connection.

Now it's time to make your commitment stronger than ever. Take the first step, and then the next. You've got this.

3

Brain Effects from Porn Addiction

The Brain Effect – My Personal Pain

Porn isn't just something you watch. It's not just a momentary escape or a harmless indulgence. It's an addiction that changes you at a fundamental level. Over time, it rewires your brain, distorts your perceptions, and makes it harder and harder to break free.

In this chapter, I'm going to dive into the profound effects porn has on the brain, and why it's so difficult to quit once it's taken hold. I'm not going to sugarcoat it. The reality of porn addiction isn't pretty, but understanding the science behind it is the first step in reclaiming your life.

The Brain on Porn: What Really Happens

Let's start with some facts. Porn is addictive, and its effects on the brain are scientifically proven. When you watch porn, your brain releases **dopamine**, a chemical that makes you feel good. It's the same chemical released when you eat something delicious, fall in love, or experience pleasure. Dopamine is what keeps you coming back for more.

But here's the kicker: with porn, the brain's reward system gets hijacked. The constant stimulation from porn doesn't just release normal amounts of dopamine—it floods your brain with excessive amounts. The more you watch, the more your brain craves that feeling, creating a cycle that becomes hard to break.

As your brain gets used to this overstimulation, it starts to **desensitize**. This means that over time, it takes more extreme or more frequent porn to feel the same rush. Your baseline of pleasure shifts. You begin to crave more—more novelty, more stimulation, more intensity—just to get the same dopamine hit. And with this escalating need for stimulation, **real life** starts to feel dull and uninteresting.

The problem is that this rewiring of your brain doesn't happen in a vacuum. It affects your **emotions**, **relationships**, and even your ability to focus and be productive. What was once a harmless habit quickly grows into an uncontrollable addiction, robbing you of time, energy, and a genuine connection with the world around you.

My Personal Pain: The Brain's Destruction in Real Time

I can't tell you how many times I promised myself that I would quit. I told myself, "This is the last time. Just one more hit of dopamine, and I'll be done." But it never worked. I'd quit for a few days, maybe even a week, but the cravings would always come back stronger.

At first, I didn't realize the effect it was having on my brain. I thought I was just dealing with a bad habit. But as I continued to indulge in porn, I started noticing the changes in my mental state.

My concentration was shot. Tasks that once seemed simple, like reading a book or focusing on work, became monumental challenges. It wasn't just that I was distracted—I was **empty**. I couldn't connect with people. I found myself feeling emotionally numb, like a shell of the person I once was.

The most painful part of this process was that I knew deep down what porn was doing to me, but I couldn't stop. I felt **trapped** in a cycle of guilt, shame, and self-loathing. It was like a part of my brain had been hijacked by the addiction, and I couldn't find my way out.

The Shame Spiral

I wasn't just battling the physical effects of addiction; I was also dealing with the emotional and psychological toll. The guilt was overwhelming. Each time I gave in to the addiction, I felt like I was betraying myself, betraying my values. I felt like a fraud. I knew I wasn't living up to the person I wanted to be, the person I was capable of being.

And the worst part? **Shame**. I felt embarrassed, isolated, and completely alone in my struggle. I would go days, sometimes weeks, without telling anyone about my struggles. I hid it, thinking that if I kept it hidden long enough, I could just control it. But the more I hid it, the worse it got.

This shame made it even harder to break free. It created a barrier between me and the world. I was ashamed of myself, of my behavior, and of the hold porn had over me. I felt like I couldn't talk to anyone because I feared they would judge me. I feared they wouldn't understand.

The Numbing Effect: Disconnecting from Life

As the addiction deepened, I felt increasingly disconnected from everything I once cared about. Porn gave me a temporary escape, but it also robbed me of true connection. I couldn't focus on relationships because my brain was focused on the constant need for more stimulation.

I noticed that I became numb to the things that used to matter. I stopped being present with my family and friends. Conversations felt hollow. My ability to feel joy or satisfaction in anything outside of porn became non-existent.

Porn created a **disconnect** between me and reality. Life didn't seem real anymore. The highs I got from porn were so intense that the simple pleasures of life—like spending time with loved ones or enjoying a good meal—felt dull. My brain was now conditioned to crave constant stimulation, and anything less felt boring.

The Turning Point: A Glimmer of Hope

At my lowest, I realized something powerful: **I couldn't keep living this way**. The pain of the addiction was starting to outweigh the temporary pleasure. I began to see the long-term consequences of my choices—not just the emotional and psychological toll, but the real, lasting damage to my relationships, my career, and my self-worth.

For the first time, I truly **understood** what porn had done to my brain. It had rewired my reward system, distorted my sense of intimacy, and created a wall between me and my true self. And as much as I was terrified of change, I knew that if I didn't break free, I would lose everything.

The pain of continuing to live in this cycle became unbearable. But there was something even more powerful than the pain: **the decision to change**.

Conclusion: Understanding the Damage and Embracing Healing

The road to recovery from porn addiction isn't easy, and the damage to the brain can take time to heal. But it's not permanent. As you read through this chapter, I want you to know that understanding the depth of the damage is the first step toward breaking free. I've been there. I've felt the shame, the numbness, the disconnection. But I've also come out on the other side. And so can you.

The brain is powerful, but it's also incredibly adaptable. You have the ability to heal, to retrain your brain, and to rediscover the life and relationships that matter most. It won't happen overnight, but with commitment, effort, and the right steps, you can **embrace your freedom** from porn—and rebuild your life from the inside out.

It's easy to get lost in the fog of addiction. For years, I was trapped in a cycle of using porn to cope with stress, boredom, and emotions I couldn't quite process. I didn't realize how deeply it was affecting my brain, my behavior, and my life. The effects were gradual at first, but over time, I noticed a shift in my thoughts, my relationships, and even my physical well-being.

In this chapter, I'll guide you through practical steps to **assess how porn is hijacking your brain** and show you **actionable steps** to start reclaiming a healthy, functioning mind. It's time to take control of your life and begin the process of rewiring your brain for freedom and fulfilment.

Step 1: Reflect on the Impact of Porn on Your Brain and Life

The first step in healing is to **acknowledge** what porn is doing to your brain. You might not realize how deeply it's affecting you until you take the time to reflect.

Here are a few questions to ask yourself as you assess the impact:

- **How often do I think about porn?** Is it consuming your thoughts throughout the day? Does it pop into your head even when you're trying to focus on other things?
- **How does porn affect my relationships?** Are you more distant, less emotionally connected, or unable to form meaningful bonds with others, especially with your partner or loved ones?
- **Do I feel numb or disconnected from real life?** Do you struggle to find joy in everyday activities, or do you feel like nothing in life excites you the way porn does?

- **How are my emotional responses?** Are you becoming more irritable, anxious, or withdrawn because of your addiction? Do you turn to porn when you're stressed or overwhelmed?

These questions are just the beginning of understanding the extent of porn's impact on your brain. It's crucial to face the truth—without judgment. Recognizing these effects is the first step to breaking free.

Step 2: Recognize the Signs of a Hijacked Brain

Porn addiction doesn't just affect your emotions and behavior—it **hijacks your brain's reward system**. Your brain starts to rely on porn for pleasure and reward, causing it to adapt in unhealthy ways.

Here's how to recognize the signs of a brain that's been hijacked by porn:

- **Increased tolerance**: Just like any other addiction, the more you consume, the more you need to get the same pleasure. If you find that the porn you watch no longer excites you as much as it used to, or you need to watch more extreme material to get the same rush, your brain has built a tolerance.
- **Difficulty focusing on anything else**: Porn addiction often comes with the inability to focus on anything but the next fix. Whether it's work, relationships, or hobbies, you might feel like you can't concentrate on anything unless it involves immediate gratification.
- **Escalating cravings**: As the addiction progresses, the cravings become more intense. You'll start finding yourself thinking about porn more often or seeking it out in situations where it would never have occurred to you before.
- **Emotional numbness**: As your brain becomes overstimulated by porn, everyday activities and interactions may seem flat. You might struggle to connect emotionally with people or experience genuine joy. Porn creates a temporary high that distorts your perception of pleasure.

By identifying these symptoms, you can begin to understand just how deeply porn has altered your brain's natural wiring.

Step 3: Set a Clear Intention to Reclaim Your Brain

The power of intention is the first step in taking back control of your mind. Once you've assessed the impact, it's time to set a **clear and firm intention** to heal. This isn't a simple decision; it's a commitment to change, to fight for your brain and your future.

By identifying these symptoms, you can begin to understand just how deeply porn has altered your brain's natural wiring.

Action Step: Write down your commitment. It could be as simple as: *"I am committed to freeing my brain from the hold of porn. I will take actionable steps every day to reclaim my focus, my joy, and my true self."*

Read this aloud every morning. Make it your affirmation. This commitment is the foundation upon which your healing will be built.

Step 4: Begin the Process of Rewiring Your Brain

Healing from porn addiction is a gradual process of **rewiring your brain**. Just like a muscle that atrophies from lack of use, your brain's reward system can be retrained to respond to healthier stimuli. This takes time, patience, and practice, but it is absolutely possible.

Here are some practical steps to begin rewiring your brain:

- **Create New Habits**: Replacing your porn habits with healthier, rewarding activities is essential. Whether it's exercising, reading, or learning a new skill, these habits will give your brain something else to crave. It won't happen overnight, but consistency is key.

- **Mindfulness and Meditation**: One of the most effective ways to reclaim control over your mind is through mindfulness practices. Meditation can help you gain awareness of your thoughts, calm your cravings, and center your mind. Even just five minutes a day can have a powerful impact.

- **Exercise and Physical Activity**: Physical exercise is not only good for your body, but it's also essential for your brain. It helps regulate emotions, increases dopamine levels in a healthier way, and gives you a natural sense of reward. Every time you choose exercise over porn, you're reinforcing the new, healthier wiring in your brain.

- **Avoid Triggers**: Part of rewiring your brain is avoiding situations that trigger your cravings. Identify the places, moments, or emotions that lead to watching porn, and create strategies to avoid or cope with them. This might involve setting up boundaries with your devices, avoiding certain situations, or seeking support when you're tempted.

- **Journaling**: Writing down your thoughts and emotions helps you process what's happening in your mind. It gives you a safe space to reflect on your feelings, recognize patterns, and track your progress. When I started journaling, I was able to understand my triggers better and manage my emotions in healthier ways.

Step 5: Seek Support and Accountability

No one should have to walk this journey alone. Porn addiction thrives in secrecy, but recovery flourishes in **connection and accountability**. You can't do it alone—you need others to help you, guide you, and hold you accountable as you rebuild your brain and your life.

Here's what you can do:

- **Find an Accountability Partner**: This could be a close friend, mentor, or even a therapist. I had a friend who was aware of my struggle, and we checked in with each other regularly. Knowing that I wasn't alone gave me strength on the days when the cravings were strongest.
- **Join a Support Group**: Whether in person or online, support groups can be a lifeline. Hearing others' stories, sharing your own struggles, and offering support to others can create a powerful sense of community. Many people in these groups have walked the same road and can provide valuable insight and encouragement.
- **Consider Professional Help**: Therapy or counselling can be incredibly beneficial for deep-rooted issues and emotional healing. A professional can help you work through the emotional pain, triggers, and thought patterns that contribute to your addiction.

Step 6: Be Patient and Compassionate with Yourself

Rewiring your brain takes time. It's not going to happen overnight. There will be setbacks, but every day that you choose to fight against the pull of porn is a victory. Healing is a journey, and it's important to be compassionate with yourself along the way.

If you slip up, don't shame yourself. Instead, use it as a learning opportunity. What led to the slip-up? What can you do differently next time? Each moment of self-awareness is another step in the right direction.

Action Step: Every evening, reflect on your day and write down **three victories**, no matter how small. Maybe you resisted the urge to watch porn, took a walk instead of retreating into isolation, or had an honest conversation with someone about your struggles. These victories will help retrain your brain to focus on success rather than failure.

Conclusion: Reclaiming Your Healthy Brain, One Step at a Time

Assessing how porn is hijacking your brain and taking actionable steps to reclaim it isn't easy, but it's the only way forward. **You can heal.** You can **rewire** your brain. You can **break free** from the chains of addiction and start living a healthier, more fulfilling life.

The key is to stay committed to the process, take one step at a time, and remain patient with yourself as you reclaim your mind. Every action, every choice, every effort you make brings you one step closer to the freedom and mental clarity you deserve.

You are not defined by your addiction. You are defined by your **strength** and your **commitment** to change.

4

Handling Urges and Relapses

Urges and Porn Relapses

When I first started my journey to quit porn, I had no idea just how powerful the urges would be. They were like waves crashing over me, each one stronger than the last, pulling me back into the same dark cycle. The cravings didn't stop just because I decided to quit; in fact, they seemed to intensify at times. Over time, I learned that managing these urges was not about fighting them directly, but about understanding where they came from and developing healthier ways to deal with them.

In this chapter, I'll share with you how I handled the urges and what caused my relapses, so you can better understand how to navigate these same challenges. Overcoming porn addiction is not a straight path. It's messy. It's tough. But with each relapse, I got a little bit stronger, a little bit wiser, and a little bit closer to the freedom I was searching for.

The Power of the Urge

Urges to watch porn are like a storm inside your mind. They come on suddenly, seemingly out of nowhere, and leave you feeling powerless. But, just like a storm, the urge eventually passes. The key is to **not act on it** and to manage the feelings it brings up.

When I felt the urge to watch porn, it wasn't just about the physical desire. It was an emotional pull. It was my brain searching for the quick dopamine fix, the escape from stress, the relief from emotional discomfort. Porn had been my coping mechanism for so long that it felt like the only way to feel better in those moments of vulnerability.

At first, I thought I could ignore it, but ignoring the urge didn't work. It only made it stronger. So, I started to shift my focus and get curious about **why** I was having these urges. This was a huge turning point for me. I realized that each urge was a signal that something was off in my emotional state or environment. The urge wasn't the problem—it was what I did with it that mattered.

My First Relapse: Understanding the Triggers

Relapses were part of my journey, and it's important to accept that setbacks do not define you. They are opportunities to **learn** and **grow**. My first relapse was a painful reminder of how much work I still needed to do.

What caused it? Looking back, I see that the relapse happened because I had stopped paying attention to my emotional needs. I had been feeling overwhelmed at work and neglected my emotional well-being. Instead of addressing the stress, I turned to porn. I convinced myself that it would bring me comfort. But instead, it left me feeling worse—guilty, ashamed, and defeated.

After the relapse, I spent some time reflecting on what went wrong. I realized that my **emotional triggers**—stress, loneliness, boredom—were the real cause. I had been ignoring my need for better self-care and emotional regulation. Porn was just the quick fix I turned to when I didn't know how to deal with these feelings.

Handling Urges: What Worked for Me

After my relapse, I decided to take a more active approach in managing the urges. I stopped seeing them as something to "fight" and instead viewed them as an opportunity to **strengthen** my emotional resilience. Here's what helped me:

1. **Pause and Breathe**

   The first thing I did when I felt the urge to watch porn was **pause**. I took a few deep breaths, focusing on the sensation of air filling my lungs and calming my nervous system. Just taking that moment to slow down helped me separate myself from the intense desire to act.

2. **Identify the Root Cause**

   Instead of trying to distract myself from the urge, I began asking myself, *"What's really going on here? Why am I feeling this way?"* Was I stressed? Lonely? Bored? Identifying the root cause gave me the clarity to understand that the urge wasn't the problem—it was the emotions I was avoiding.

3. **Distraction with Purpose**

   When I felt the urge to act on porn, I replaced it with an activity that gave me real satisfaction and focus. For me, it was exercising, reading, or even calling a friend. I started to develop a **toolbox** of activities that were not just distractions, but **meaningful alternatives**. These activities gave me a natural dopamine boost and helped me feel good without resorting to porn.

4. **Mindfulness and Meditation**

   Practicing mindfulness helped me become more aware of my thoughts and cravings. By observing the urge without judgment, I started to notice how quickly it came and went. I realized that **urges are temporary**. They don't last forever, and the more I practiced sitting with them instead of acting on them, the less power they had over me.

5. **Accountability**

I also found that being accountable to someone else was incredibly helpful. Sharing my struggles with a close friend or mentor helped me stay committed to my journey. It made the process less isolating and helped me feel supported when the cravings were at their peak.

The Cycle of Relapse and Recovery

I want to be real with you: relapses don't just happen once—they can happen multiple times on this journey. The most important thing I learned is that a **relapse doesn't mean failure**. It's a signal that something in your approach needs to change. For me, each relapse taught me something valuable about my triggers and how to handle them better next time.

The key is to not give up. It's easy to feel defeated, but the truth is, recovery isn't a straight line. It's a winding road with bumps and detours, but every step forward counts. When I relapsed, I didn't quit trying. I simply **adjusted** my strategy and tried again. The more I did this, the more resilient I became.

Building Long-Term Resilience

As I continued on my journey, I noticed something remarkable: the urges became **less frequent** and **less intense** over time. My brain was starting to rewire itself. I was no longer seeking porn to cope with my emotions. Instead, I had developed healthier ways to manage stress, loneliness, and boredom.

Building long-term resilience came down to creating a lifestyle that **supported** my recovery. This meant making sure I was **physically active, emotionally engaged**, and **socially connected**. I also made it a priority to practice self-compassion and give myself grace when I stumbled. I didn't beat myself up; instead, I acknowledged my growth and kept moving forward.

The Key Takeaways:

- **Urges are temporary**—they come and go. With practice, you'll learn to sit with them and let them pass.
- **Emotional triggers**—stress, loneliness, and boredom—are often at the root of the urge to watch porn. Addressing these emotions is key to long-term success.
- **Healthy coping strategies**—exercising, connecting with others, journaling, or meditating—can replace the need for porn.
- **Accountability** is a powerful tool for staying committed. Share your journey with someone who can support you.
- **Relapses are part of the process**—they are opportunities for growth, not failure. Learn from them and keep moving forward.

Moving Forward: Freedom from the Urge

The road to freedom isn't about eliminating the urges completely - it's about developing the strength to **choose differently** when they arise. I won't lie and say that I never experience a craving, but I've learned how to manage them and understand that I have the power to choose my response.

Every day you resist the urge to fall back into old patterns is a victory. Every step you take toward healing and understanding yourself better makes you stronger. You are in control, not the urges.

Keep going. You're closer to freedom than you think.

Action: Steps to Breaking Urges and Relapses

When I first decided to quit porn, I had a naive belief that once I made the decision, it would be smooth sailing. Unfortunately, the reality hit hard. The urges to watch porn came on strong, and the temptation often felt unbearable. What I didn't know at the time was that beating these urges and avoiding relapse would require much more than just willpower—it would take real, practical steps, consistent effort, and a deep understanding of myself.

In this chapter, I'm going to share the real, raw steps that helped me navigate my addiction. I want you to know that overcoming urges and preventing relapses is not about perfection. It's about learning how to deal with the challenges as they come and, ultimately, creating a life where porn no longer has a hold on you.

Understanding the Urge

Before we get into the practical steps, it's important to understand what you're dealing with when an urge to watch porn arises. The craving isn't just a random thought; it's your brain reaching for a quick dopamine fix. The addiction to porn is deeply rooted in the brain's reward system. Porn delivers an intense rush of pleasure, and your brain starts to associate it with relief from stress, boredom, loneliness, or anxiety.

Over time, the brain starts to crave that quick fix. That's why the urge to watch porn feels so powerful. But here's the thing: **the urge doesn't control you. You control your actions.**

Step 1: Recognize the Urge and Pause

The first thing you need to do when you feel the urge to watch porn is to **recognize it**. It's easy to ignore it or brush it off, but recognizing it for what it is—a temporary craving—is the first step in beating it.

When the urge hit me, I used to go into autopilot and allow myself to follow the path. But after some reflection, I realized that I needed to take a pause before acting. So now, when the urge hits, I stop for a moment. I take a deep breath, and I remind myself: "This is temporary. It will pass."

Why this works: When you pause, you take a moment to break the cycle. You give yourself space between the trigger and the action. And in that space, you reclaim control.

Step 2: Identify the Trigger

Every urge to watch porn has a **trigger**. For me, the triggers were often stress, boredom, or moments when I felt emotionally drained. It wasn't always about lust or sexual desire—it was about trying to escape something uncomfortable in my life.

Ask yourself: *What just happened? What am I feeling right now?*

Is it stress from work? Loneliness? Anxiety about something in your life?

Once I identified my triggers, I started to **address the underlying emotion** instead of reaching for porn to numb it. For example, if I felt stressed, I would go for a walk, call a friend, or do something creative. If I was feeling bored, I would immerse myself in a hobby or get out of the house.

Why this works: When you address the emotional trigger directly, you stop using porn as a coping mechanism. Instead, you learn healthier ways to deal with the uncomfortable emotions.

Step 3: Replace the Habit with Something Positive

When you quit porn, there's an emotional void left behind. You can't simply stop watching porn without replacing it with something else—something that fulfills you in a healthy, meaningful way. **Find something that gives you the same dopamine boost** but without the damaging effects.

For me, I started working out more regularly. Exercise became a way to deal with stress, anxiety, and any other negative feelings that might trigger the urge. Whether it was lifting weights, going for a run, or practicing yoga, the physical activity helped regulate my emotions and gave me something positive to focus on.

Why this works: Replacing the habit with something healthier is key to rewiring your brain. When your brain is used to getting a dopamine boost from porn, you have to retrain it to get that boost from something positive—something that builds you up rather than tearing you down.

Step 4: Mindfulness and Self-Compassion

Mindfulness was one of the most important tools I used to stop porn addiction. Instead of just reacting to the urge, I learned to observe it without judgment. Mindfulness taught me to acknowledge the urge as a passing thought rather than something I had to act on.

Self-compassion was another big piece of the puzzle. I used to beat myself up every time I relapsed. The guilt and shame would pile on, making the problem feel even bigger. But I realized that **self-judgment**

only fuels the addiction. When I made a mistake, I treated myself with kindness and reminded myself that this was a journey.

Why this works: Mindfulness helps you observe your thoughts and emotions without being controlled by them. Self-compassion helps you bounce back from setbacks without spiraling into guilt or shame.

Step 5: Set Clear Goals and Track Your Progress

One of the most effective ways I stayed on track was by setting **clear, actionable goals**. Instead of just saying, "I'm going to quit porn," I broke it down into smaller, manageable milestones. I started with 24 hours without porn, then 3 days, then a week. Each time I reached a goal, I celebrated it, no matter how small.

Tracking my progress kept me focused on the positive changes I was making, rather than the times I slipped. It helped me see that I was, in fact, moving forward, even when things felt tough.

Why this works: When you set goals and track your progress, you build momentum. Each victory, no matter how small, becomes evidence that you can keep going.

Step 6: Accountability and Support

When I tried to do this alone, I found myself isolated and vulnerable. But once I started **opening up** to someone about my struggle, it made all the difference. Whether it was a close friend, a support group, or a mentor, having someone who knew about my journey and who I could talk to made it much easier to stay committed.

Accountability isn't just about telling someone when you've messed up; it's about having someone who can remind you of your strength when you feel weak. It's someone who can offer encouragement, perspective, and the reassurance that you're not alone.

Why this works: Accountability gives you a sense of connection and responsibility. It's harder to relapse when you know someone is rooting for you.

Step 7: Prepare for Relapses—And Learn From Them

Relapses are part of the process. I don't want to sugarcoat it—there will be times when you slip up. It's important not to see these relapses as the end of your journey but as an opportunity to learn. Every time I relapsed, I looked for the lessons. What triggered me? What could I do differently next time?

It's about **progress, not perfection**. Each relapse was an opportunity to better understand myself, my triggers, and my needs.

Why this works: When you prepare for setbacks and view them as lessons, you don't let them derail your progress. Instead, you use them as stepping stones on the path to lasting change.

Step 8: Practice Self-Discipline Every Day

Discipline isn't about forcing yourself into compliance; it's about consistently choosing your future over the temporary pleasure of porn. Every day, I made the conscious decision to **put in the work** to build a life I wanted. It wasn't always easy, but the more I practiced self-discipline, the easier it became to say no to porn.

Why this works: Self-discipline is like a muscle—it gets stronger the more you use it. The more you choose healthier habits, the less power porn has over you.

Conclusion

Beating porn addiction isn't easy. But it's not impossible. By recognizing the urge, identifying triggers, replacing old habits, practicing mindfulness, seeking support, and preparing for setbacks, you can reclaim control over your life. It's a process, and it's one you can absolutely navigate.

Take it one day at a time. Celebrate your victories, no matter how small. And remember: you are **stronger** than the urges. You are **in control**. Keep moving forward, and freedom will be yours.

5

Breaking the Chains of Porn Addiction

Breaking Free from Porn

The Science Behind Addiction: Why Porn is So Hard to Quit

When it comes to quitting porn, many men face an uphill battle. It's not just a matter of willpower or self-discipline—it's about the way our brains work. The science of addiction can help explain why porn is so hard to quit and why it feels like a constant struggle to break free.

At the core of addiction is **dopamine**, a chemical in your brain that's responsible for feelings of pleasure and reward. When you watch porn, your brain releases a huge rush of dopamine, creating an intense feeling of satisfaction. This rush is similar to what happens when you eat a favorite food, exercise, or achieve something important. The problem is that porn gives you an artificial and overwhelming dopamine boost, which sets up a cycle of craving. Your brain starts associating porn with pleasure, which leads to wanting more of it—again and again.

But here's the catch: over time, the brain starts to adapt. The more you engage in porn use, the more your brain needs that same intense stimulation to get the same reward. This is known as **tolerance**—and it's why you might find yourself watching more, seeking out more extreme content, or feeling like the satisfaction isn't lasting anymore. It becomes harder to stop because the brain gets wired to crave the high.

Breaking free from porn isn't just about stopping a habit—it's about rewiring your brain to respond differently to triggers and cravings. This process takes time and effort, but it's completely possible with the right approach.

A Multi-Step Approach: Self-Awareness, Habit Replacement, and Emotional Regulation

The journey to quitting porn is a multi-step process, and understanding the science behind addiction is just the beginning. To successfully quit, you need to approach it in a way that addresses both the mental and emotional aspects of the addiction.

Here's a simple framework to follow:

1. **Self-Awareness:**

   The first step in breaking any habit is becoming aware of it. You need to identify when and why you turn to porn. Is it triggered by stress, boredom, loneliness, or something else? Keep track of your thoughts and feelings when you're tempted. Awareness is the foundation of change—it's about understanding what's happening in your mind and body when the urge arises.

2. **Habit Replacement:**

   Once you're aware of the triggers, you can start replacing the habit of watching porn with healthier activities. It's not enough just to stop. You need to create new routines, hobbies, and interests that give you the same sense of fulfilment and enjoyment. Whether it's exercise, creative projects, reading, or spending time with loved ones, find activities that help you cope with stress and give you joy.

3. **Emotional Regulation:**

   One of the hardest parts of quitting porn is managing the emotional ups and downs that come with it. Porn often serves as a way to escape negative emotions like anxiety, shame, or sadness. When you take away the coping mechanism of porn, you need to develop new ways of dealing with those emotions. Emotional regulation is about learning to sit with discomfort and find healthier ways to process your feelings. It might involve practicing mindfulness, journaling, or simply giving yourself permission to feel without immediately reacting.

Managing Cravings and Avoiding Relapse: Step-by-Step Guidance

Cravings will happen. That's a fact. It's important to be prepared for them, so you don't feel defeated when they arise. Here are some simple, actionable steps to help you manage cravings and avoid relapse:

1. **Pause and Breathe:**

   When you feel the urge to watch porn, stop what you're doing and take a few deep breaths. Inhale slowly, hold, and then exhale. This helps calm your nervous system and gives you a moment to interrupt the craving.

2. **Change Your Environment:**

   Cravings often arise when we're in certain places or situations. If you're alone, tired, or bored, the temptation to watch porn may be stronger. Change your environment: go for a walk, grab a snack, or do something that distracts you and moves you out of the situation.

3. **Engage Your Mind:**

   The best way to break a craving is by redirecting your focus. Pick up a book, watch an inspiring video, or call a friend. The goal is to do something that demands your attention and pulls you away from the temptation.

4. **Use Your "Why"**:

   Remember why you're quitting in the first place. Review your list of reasons why you want to be free from porn. When you feel the urge to relapse, remind yourself of the bigger picture—your health, your relationships, your future. Keep that vision in mind to stay motivated.

5. **Get Accountability**:

   Don't try to do this alone. Find someone you trust—whether it's a mentor, a therapist, or a support group—and check in regularly. Having someone who holds you accountable makes it harder to slip back into old habits.

Mindfulness, Meditation, and Self-Reflection: Tools for Healing

Mindfulness and meditation are powerful tools that can help you stay grounded throughout your journey of quitting. These practices help you build self-awareness, regulate your emotions, and manage cravings.

- **Mindfulness** is the practice of being fully present in the moment, without judgment. It helps you become more aware of your thoughts and feelings, and allows you to observe them without getting caught up in them. When you feel the urge to watch porn, mindfulness can help you pause and notice the craving without reacting to it. This gives you a moment of choice—the ability to decide whether or not to act on the urge.

- **Meditation** is a practice that helps you train your mind to focus and calm your thoughts. Even just a few minutes of meditation each day can help reduce stress, improve focus, and increase your emotional resilience. Guided meditations specifically focused on addiction recovery can be especially helpful.

- **Self-Reflection** is essential for healing. Journaling or taking time to reflect on your thoughts and progress can help you stay on track. By reflecting on your journey, you can celebrate your small victories and learn from your setbacks.

Replacing the Empty Time – Finding New Hobbies and Interests

When you quit porn, there's often a void left in your life. The time you used to spend on watching porn can now be filled with something else—something that adds real value to your life. This is a great opportunity to discover new hobbies, interests, and passions.

- **Exercise**:

    Physical activity is one of the best ways to release built-up tension and boost your mood. Whether it's going for a run, lifting weights, or doing yoga, exercise gives you a natural high that can replace the dopamine rush you used to get from porn.

- **Creative Pursuits**:

    Engage in something creative, like painting, writing, playing music, or photography. Creative hobbies are not only rewarding, but they also help you express yourself in ways that build your confidence and sense of purpose.

- **Social Activities**:

    Spend more time with family and friends. Building stronger connections and enjoying meaningful conversations will help you feel more fulfilled and less isolated.

- **Personal Development**:

    Use this time to improve yourself. Read books, take up online courses, or work on building new skills. This is your chance to invest in the person you want to become.

The Power of Accountability – Finding Support

Quitting porn isn't something you should do alone. Having accountability can make all the difference. Whether you turn to a mentor, a therapist, or a support group, sharing your struggles and victories with someone else will keep you on track.

- **Mentors**:

    A mentor is someone who has walked the path you're on. They can offer guidance, support, and encouragement as you work through your challenges.

- **Therapists**:

    A therapist can help you dig deeper into the emotional and psychological aspects of your addiction. They provide a safe space to explore your triggers and develop strategies for healing.

- **Support Groups**:

    There are many support groups, both online and in-person, that focus on helping men quit porn. These groups provide a sense of community, where you can share your experiences and learn from others who are going through the same journey.

Rewiring Your Brain: Consistency, Discipline, and Small Victories

Rewiring your brain is a process that takes time. But with consistent practice, discipline, and a focus on small victories, you can create lasting change. Every time you make the decision to say "no" to porn, you strengthen your ability to resist the next time. Every day you stay committed, your brain begins to adapt. The cravings will get weaker, the temptation will lessen, and you'll feel more in control.

Remember, change doesn't happen overnight. But if you stick to your plan, practice new habits, and stay accountable, you'll start to see real transformation. And each small victory is a step closer to the life you want to live.

Conclusion: The Power Is in Your Hands

The road to quitting porn is challenging, but it is also incredibly rewarding. By understanding the science behind addiction, practicing mindfulness, developing new habits, and staying accountable, you're giving yourself the tools to succeed. You have the power to rewire your brain and reclaim your life. The journey starts today. Take it one step at a time, and trust that you're capable of more than you think.

Action: Breaking the Chains of Porn Addiction

When I was stuck in the cycle of porn addiction, I kept waiting for the day when I would magically wake up free from the cravings, free from the shame, and free from the pull of addiction. But that day never came until I took real action. I had to make a choice. I had to take responsibility for my own recovery. And I had to act.

Quitting porn isn't about willpower alone; it's about taking **practical steps** that set you up for success. It's about creating new habits, managing emotions, and finding healthier ways to deal with cravings. It's also about surrounding yourself with the right people and building a support system. I can tell you from experience, it's possible to break free. Let me walk you through the action steps that helped me—and can help you—create lasting change.

1. What New Habits Can I Adopt?

One of the hardest things about breaking a porn addiction is the **habit** of reaching for it when I was bored, stressed, or feeling down. I had to **replace** those old habits with healthier ones. This isn't a quick fix; it's a long-term strategy for reprogramming your brain. Here's what worked for me:

- **Morning Routines:**

    I started every morning by doing something productive. It could be something as simple as making my bed or drinking a glass of water. Having a clear morning routine gave me a sense of accomplishment right from the start and helped me feel in control of my day.

- **Exercise:**

    I incorporated physical activity into my daily routine. Whether it was a morning jog, a few sets of push-ups, or just stretching, exercise became a healthy outlet for the energy that used to go into watching porn. It also helped regulate my mood and reduce stress.

- **Mindfulness Practices:**

    I began practicing mindfulness meditation. Just a few minutes each day helped me become more aware of my thoughts and feelings without acting on them. It allowed me to pause, reflect, and make better choices, especially when cravings hit.

- **Reading and Learning:**

    I replaced my screen time with reading. I started with books that inspired me, self-help books, and anything that could help me grow as a person.

Filling my mind with positive and productive content made me feel more fulfilled and less likely to turn to porn for relief.

2. How Can I Control My Emotions?

One of the biggest reasons I turned to porn in the first place was to cope with **emotions**—stress, loneliness, frustration, and even boredom. It was an easy escape, but it was never a lasting solution. Over time, I learned that the key to breaking free wasn't avoiding emotions, but **learning how to manage them**.

Here's what I did:

- **Emotional Awareness:**

    I started paying attention to my emotions. I would ask myself, "What am I feeling right now?" and "Why do I feel this way?" Often, I realized I was turning to porn as a way to avoid feeling sad, stressed, or anxious. Once I recognized my triggers, I could address them head-on.

- **Journaling:**

    Writing down my thoughts and feelings became an outlet for processing my emotions. When I felt overwhelmed, I would take a few minutes to journal. This helped me work through difficult emotions without resorting to old habits.

- **Deep Breathing:**

    When I felt a craving coming on or was overwhelmed by negative emotions, I practiced deep breathing. Inhaling deeply for four seconds, holding it for four seconds, and then exhaling for four seconds helped calm my body and mind. It gave me the space I needed to think clearly and not act impulsively.

3. How Can I Manage Cravings?

Cravings are going to come. That's a fact. But what I realized is that **cravings don't last forever**. I needed to have a game plan for how to deal with them when they hit. Here's what worked for me:

- **Pause and Breathe:**

  When a craving came on, I didn't try to fight it. I simply paused. I took a deep breath and reminded myself that cravings are temporary. I would tell myself, "This feeling will pass. I'm in control."

- **Distraction:**

  I would **distract myself** with something engaging. I'd grab a book, call a friend, or even go outside for a walk. The key was to change my focus and redirect my energy.

- **Mindful Awareness:**

  I also practiced mindfulness during cravings. I would pay attention to what was going on in my body and mind without judgment. "I feel the urge to watch porn. I feel anxious. I feel frustrated." Just acknowledging the craving without reacting to it made it easier to manage.

- **Count to 10:**

  One simple trick I used was to count to 10 when a craving hit. By slowing things down and taking a moment, I gave myself the chance to think before acting.

4. What New Hobbies Can I Have?

One of the biggest challenges of quitting porn was the **empty time** it left. I realized that I needed to replace the hours I spent consuming porn with something productive, fulfilling, and enjoyable. This is where new hobbies came into play.

Here's what I did:

- **Exercise:**

  I mentioned this earlier, but it bears repeating. Exercise was my go-to hobby. Not only did it improve my physical health, but it also boosted my mental health and gave me a natural high that kept me away from porn.

- **Creative Outlets:**

  I started painting, writing, and playing the guitar. These creative activities gave me a sense of accomplishment and helped me tap into emotions in a healthy way. It was amazing how much my self-esteem grew when I realized I could create something beautiful with my hands.

- **Learning and Growth:**

  I began reading books, taking online courses, and watching educational videos. These hobbies gave me purpose and made me feel like I was investing in myself, instead of wasting time.

- **Socializing:**

  I made a point to spend more time with friends and family. We all need connection, and being around people who care about me helped me feel supported and less isolated.

5. Who Can I Have as an Accountability Partner?

I can't stress this enough—**accountability** is a game-changer. The support of someone you trust is invaluable on this journey. I knew I couldn't do this alone, so I reached out for help.

- **Friends or Family:**

  I confided in a close friend who knew what I was going through. He became my accountability partner, someone who would check in with me regularly. Just knowing that someone was holding me accountable made a huge difference.

- **Therapists:**

  I worked with a therapist to explore the emotional and psychological reasons behind my addiction. Therapy helped me unpack deep-seated feelings and patterns that I couldn't have done alone.

- **Support Groups:**

  I also joined an online support group for men dealing with porn addiction. These groups offered a sense of community and understanding. I could share my victories and setbacks with others who truly understood what I was going through.

6. What Practical Steps Can I Take to Improve Self-Discipline?

Building self-discipline was a critical part of my recovery. I knew that to break free, I had to stay committed even when things got tough. Here are the practical steps I used to improve my self-discipline:

- **Set Clear Goals:**

  I set specific goals, such as "I will go 30 days without watching porn." Having a clear target gave me something to work toward. Once I reached a goal, I would set a new one. Each success motivated me to keep going.

- **Create Routines:**

  I built strong, healthy routines. I didn't leave room for impulse decisions. My daily routine involved exercise, self-reflection, work, and healthy leisure activities. Routines created structure, which made it easier to stay disciplined.

- **Reward Myself:**

    I celebrated small victories. After a week of no porn, I treated myself to something special. Whether it was a movie night or a new book, giving myself rewards helped keep me motivated.

- **Stay Consistent:**

    Discipline is built on consistency. I kept working on my goals, day in and day out, even when it felt tough. I knew that every small action added up to lasting change

---

Conclusion: The Power of Practical Action

Breaking free from porn addiction is no easy feat, but I want you to know that **it is possible**. It's about taking practical, actionable steps to break the chains that hold you back. From adopting new habits and managing emotions to building accountability and improving self-discipline, every step you take brings you closer to the life you deserve.

You have the power to make real change. I did it, and so can you.

Take action today. Start small, stay consistent, and trust the process. You are capable of living a life free from the chains of porn addiction.

6

Rebuilding Your Life After Porn

Rebuilding Your Life: The Journey Starts

In this final chapter, we'll explore the transformative power of living authentically and confidently in every area of your life. From Overcoming porn addiction isn't just about stopping a behavior. It's about healing the emotional scars that addiction leaves behind. It's about **regaining your sense of self-worth, overcoming guilt and shame**, and **rebuilding trust in yourself**. The path to true freedom goes beyond the physical act—it's about emotional healing and reconnecting with the life you want to live. I know this because I've walked that path.

When I first began this journey, I didn't just feel stuck in my addiction—I felt completely broken. I had hurt myself, disappointed the people who cared about me, and lost touch with the man I once hoped to be. Healing these wounds took time, effort, and patience. But I want to share with you what I've learned, so you can begin the process of rebuilding your life too.

1. Regaining Self-Worth

When you're addicted to porn, it's easy to fall into a cycle of **self-loathing**. The guilt and shame can make you feel worthless. I felt like I was unworthy of success, love, or happiness. I thought I was weak because I couldn't control my urges. But here's what I realized: **Addiction does not define your worth**.

The first step in healing is to remind yourself that you are worthy of change. You deserve happiness, peace, and a healthy life. But it starts with believing in your own **value** again.

Here's what helped me:

- **Self-Compassion**:

  I learned to treat myself with kindness. Instead of beating myself up for past mistakes, I forgave myself. Healing starts when you show yourself the same compassion you would show to a friend who is struggling.

- **Positive Affirmations**:

  Every day, I told myself something positive. It was simple at first: "I am worthy of love. I am worthy of change." It may sound small, but those affirmations began to rewire my brain and boost my self-esteem.

- **Focus on Progress, Not Perfection**:

  I stopped expecting immediate perfection. I celebrated the small victories, knowing they would add up over time. Each step forward, no matter how small, proved that I was capable of change.

2. Overcoming Guilt and Shame

Guilt and shame are two of the most powerful emotions that addiction fosters. I was constantly haunted by the **regret** of my actions and the **shame** of what I had done. It wasn't just about the addiction itself—it was the feelings of failure and unworthiness that followed.

But healing from guilt and shame involves **acknowledging** what happened, accepting responsibility, and then **forgiving yourself**. Yes, you made mistakes. Yes, you've hurt others. But that doesn't mean you are beyond redemption.

What worked for me:

- **Acknowledging the Hurt**:

  I had to face the reality of how my addiction had affected my life and the lives of those around me. This wasn't easy, but it helped me to take ownership of my actions without falling into self-blame.

- **Letting Go of Perfectionism**:

  I had to accept that I couldn't change the past, and I needed to let go of the idea that I could be perfect moving forward. **Progress, not perfection**, became my mantra.

- **Seeking Forgiveness**:

  I also sought forgiveness from others when I could. I wasn't expecting them to erase the past, but offering an apology was a part of my healing process. It helped to release some of the burden of guilt and allowed me to move forward with integrity.

3. Rebuilding Trust in Yourself

One of the hardest things to rebuild after addiction is **trust in yourself**. When you repeatedly break your promises to yourself, it's hard to believe you can actually change. I had made so many promises to quit, only to fall back into old habits. But regaining trust in yourself is possible.

Here's how I did it:

- **Small Wins**:

  Every time I kept a promise to myself, no matter how small, I celebrated it. Over time, those small wins built my confidence and reminded me that I was capable of sticking to my word.

- **Setting Boundaries**:

  I set clear boundaries for myself—both physically and mentally. I avoided situations that would trigger my cravings and reminded myself of the goals I had set. When I stuck to my boundaries, I began to trust myself again.

- **Consistency**

  Trusting yourself means showing up for yourself day after day. It's about building a consistent routine that reinforces your commitment to change. Over time, consistency will help rebuild that trust.

4. Restoring Damaged Relationships

One of the most difficult parts of addiction is the damage it causes to the relationships that matter most. Family, partners, friends—they all feel the effects. And it's hard to know where to begin when it comes to mending those relationships. But it is possible, and I want to share how I did it.

Here's what helped me:

- **Honest Communication**:

  I started by being honest about my struggles. I didn't make excuses, and I didn't try to downplay the situation. I told my loved ones what I was going through and asked for their support. This honesty was hard, but it helped rebuild trust.

- **Accountability**:

  I worked on being accountable, not just to myself, but to the people I loved. I kept them informed of my progress, setbacks, and how I was handling my recovery. It showed them that I was serious about change.

- **Patience**:

  Relationships take time to rebuild. I had to be patient with myself and with others. Healing wasn't immediate, and I had to earn back the trust that I had lost.

- **Setting New Boundaries**:

  I made sure to set new boundaries to protect my relationships. This meant creating space for open communication, being emotionally available, and avoiding situations that would cause further harm.

5. Building Healthy, Meaningful Connections

As I healed, I realized that the **quality of my relationships** mattered more than the number of friends I had. I started to prioritize relationships that brought out the best in me and allowed me to be my true self.

- **Building a Support Network**:

  I surrounded myself with people who encouraged my growth, rather than people who enabled my old habits. I sought out mentors, friends, and groups who understood my journey and were willing to support me.

- **Vulnerability**:

  I allowed myself to be vulnerable with others, sharing my struggles and triumphs. Opening up in this way built deeper connections with those who truly cared about me.

- **Healthy Communication**:

  I learned how to communicate my needs, feelings, and boundaries in a healthy way. This allowed me to build stronger, more meaningful relationships moving forward.

6. Reconnecting with Your Passions, Dreams, and Purpose

Quitting porn wasn't just about breaking a bad habit—it was about rediscovering the man I had lost along the way. During my recovery, I took the time to reconnect with the things I used to love.

I thought about what I wanted for my life, beyond the addiction. What did I truly care about? What made me excited? What was my purpose?

I started small:

- I revisited old passions: painting, writing, and music. These activities had been pushed aside for years, but they became a powerful source of fulfilment during my recovery.

- I set new goals: These were goals I could work toward every day. Whether it was fitness-related, career-focused, or personal development goals, having something to strive for kept me motivated.

- I found meaning in my journey: I realized that overcoming this addiction was part of my larger purpose. I wanted to help others who were struggling. That sense of **purpose** became a driving force in my life.

7. Setting New Goals and Creating a Vision for the Future

Now that I had regained some clarity, I set a vision for my future. I knew that if I didn't have clear goals, I would fall back into old patterns.

- I started setting **long-term** and **short-term** goals. The long-term goals gave me something to look forward to, and the short-term goals gave me momentum.

- I created a vision for who I wanted to become and what I wanted to achieve. It gave me focus and determination. Every small step was part of a larger picture.

- I made sure that my goals were aligned with my values—things like personal growth, family, and helping others.

8. The Importance of Daily Routines

Lastly, I realized that **daily routines** were critical for long-term recovery. Without structure, I would fall back into old habits. I had to build a life that supported my recovery every day.

Here's what my routine looked like:

- **Morning Rituals**:

    I started each day with a morning ritual that included meditation, stretching, and setting my intentions for the day.

- **Consistent Habits**:

    I made exercise, reading, and journaling non-negotiable parts of my day.

- **Evening Reflections**:

    At night, I would reflect on my day—what went well, what I could improve, and how I was progressing in my recovery.

Final Thought

Rebuilding your life after addiction is a process. It's not easy, but it is worth it. You can heal your emotional wounds, restore your relationships, and reconnect with your purpose. It's about setting a new course for your future, and most importantly, making a commitment to yourself that you are worthy of a better life.

The man you've always wanted to be is still inside you. You just need to believe it - and take the steps to reclaim him.

7

Embracing Freedom from Porn

A Learning Journey About True Masculinity

There is something powerful about reaching the point where you can truly say, "I'm free." For years, porn had a grip on my life. It shaped my choices, clouded my thoughts, and kept me from living the life I wanted. But today, I stand here—proud of my freedom, proud of the resilience and discipline I built, and proud of the man I've become.

In this chapter, I'll share how I embraced my freedom from porn, and how you can too. Freedom isn't just about quitting porn—it's about **transforming your mindset, taking control of your life, and developing a continuous growth mentality**.

1. The Mindset of a Man Who is Free

When I first quit porn, there was an immediate sense of relief. But over time, I realized that freedom wasn't just about **stopping** something. It was about **becoming** someone new.

The man I became was strong, resilient, and disciplined. I wasn't defined by my past or my addiction—I was defined by the decisions I made each day to live a better life.

How to develop the mindset of a man who is free:

- **Celebrate Your Strength:**

    Every time you resist a craving or stay on course, recognize your strength. I started seeing myself as a strong man who had conquered something difficult. I took pride in the fact that I didn't give up on myself, even when it felt hard. This shift in mindset helped me embrace my freedom more fully.

- **Recognize Your Resilience:**

    Addiction isn't easy to overcome. There were days when I wanted to give up, but I pushed through. I reminded myself of the resilience I had. **You're stronger than you realize.** Every time you face a challenge and overcome it, you build resilience. And that resilience is what will keep you free.

- **Discipline is Freedom:**

    The discipline I learned through quitting porn became one of the most valuable tools I carry with me today. Maintaining my freedom requires the same discipline that helped me quit in the first place. Staying committed to healthy habits, self-care, and emotional regulation became second nature.

2. Maintaining Long-Term Progress: The Mindset of Continuous Growth

The journey doesn't stop the moment you quit. Freedom isn't a one-time event; it's a continual process. A **growth mindset** is essential if you want to maintain progress long-term. Overcoming addiction isn't the end—it's just the beginning.

To stay free, I realized that I needed to continue growing as a person. I had to embrace challenges as opportunities to **learn** and **develop** further.

How to cultivate a mindset of continuous growth:

- **Embrace New Challenges**:

  Once I quit porn, I set new goals for myself. I wasn't content to just quit—I wanted to be better in every aspect of my life. Whether it was my career, my relationships, or my personal health, I pushed myself to continue growing. Every new challenge became a chance to build upon my success.

- **Celebrate Progress, Not Perfection**:

  Progress doesn't mean perfection. There were times when I made mistakes or faced setbacks, but I learned to see those moments as part of the journey. Every day I stayed free was a win. Focusing on my progress kept me motivated to keep going.

- **Create a Plan for Continuous Improvement**:

  I realized that to stay free, I needed to build a life that supported my long-term success. That meant surrounding myself with healthy influences, prioritizing my well-being, and committing to continuous self-improvement.

3. The Importance of Self-Care and Emotional Regulation

One of the most important things I learned on my journey was that true freedom requires **self-care**. I used to neglect my emotional needs, thinking that simply quitting porn would solve everything. But I soon realized that to maintain my freedom, I needed to **nurture myself**, both physically and emotionally.

Practical steps for maintaining emotional well-being:

- **Regular Exercise**: Physical health and mental health are connected. I started exercising regularly to release pent-up energy and reduce stress. Exercise not only improved my physical health but also helped me regulate my emotions and maintain focus.

- **Mindfulness and Meditation**: Learning to regulate my emotions through mindfulness and meditation became essential. These practices helped me stay calm in moments of stress and gave me the mental clarity I needed to make good decisions.
- **Healthy Outlets for Emotions**: Porn was a coping mechanism for many of my emotional struggles. Once I let go of that, I had to find healthier ways to manage my emotions. I took up journaling, deep breathing exercises, and talked to friends when I felt overwhelmed. Finding healthy outlets is essential for long-term freedom.

4. Stories of Men Who Have Transformed Their Lives

There were times when I felt like I was the only one struggling. But then, I met men who had gone through the same journey and emerged stronger and more fulfilled. Their stories gave me hope and showed me that **change is possible** for anyone who is committed to the process.

One man I met had been struggling with porn for nearly a decade. He shared how his addiction impacted his marriage, his self-esteem, and his sense of purpose. But after he made the decision to quit, he transformed his life. He went from being isolated and depressed to becoming a loving husband and father, and he reconnected with his passion for writing. His story inspired me to keep going, and I know it can inspire you too.

There are countless men who have made the same decision to quit and have completely transformed their lives. Whether it's through regaining their relationships, boosting their careers, or reconnecting with their passions, these stories are proof that **freedom from porn is possible**.

5. Overcoming Relapse and Dealing with Future Challenges

As much as I'd like to say that quitting porn was a one-time event and that I've never been tempted again, the truth is, the journey isn't linear. There were moments when I felt weak, when cravings crept up, or when life felt overwhelming. But I had learned to **deal with challenges** and **prevent relapse** by relying on the lessons I'd learned.

Steps to prevent relapse and handle future challenges:

- **Stay Aware of Triggers**: Understanding my triggers was key. I learned that certain emotions—stress, boredom, or loneliness—could trigger cravings. By being aware of these triggers, I could take action to prevent them from taking control.
- **Develop an Emergency Plan**: I created an emergency plan for moments when I felt the urge to relapse. This plan included steps like distracting myself with a hobby, talking to an accountability partner, or going for a walk. Knowing what to do in these moments helped me avoid giving in.
- **Continue Your Growth Journey**: The most important thing I did was to **never stop growing**. Whenever I faced a challenge, I reminded myself of all the progress I had made. Every setback was an opportunity to strengthen my resolve.

Final Thoughts: Freedom is a Lifelong Journey

Embracing my freedom from porn addiction didn't happen overnight. It's been a gradual process, built on strength, resilience, and discipline. But now, looking back, I can honestly say that I'm proud of who I've become.

Overcoming addiction isn't just about quitting; it's about continuing the journey of self-mastery. It's about committing to your **growth**, taking care of your **emotional well-being**, and **never giving up** on yourself.

Remember: **Freedom is not a destination; it's a way of life**. You can live that life too. Stay focused on your growth, practice self-care, and never stop believing in your ability to create the life you deserve. You have the strength within you to continue this journey and embrace the freedom that's waiting for you.

Action: Embrace the New You

Freedom from porn isn't just about saying goodbye to something toxic. It's about stepping into a new life, a new version of yourself—one that is healthier, more fulfilled, and ready to take on the world. But this transformation doesn't happen by itself. You have to make it happen, day by day, step by step.

As someone who has walked this path, I know what it feels like to want to quit but not know where to start. I understand the battle with cravings, the fear of relapse, and the confusion about how to live without the crutch of porn. But let me tell you this: the freedom you crave is achievable, and it starts with **practical, actionable steps** that you can begin today.

In this section, I'll share the steps I took and you can take to embrace my freedom. These are real actions that require effort, but they will lead to real change.

1. Commit to a Clear Decision: "I Am Done with Porn"

The first step in embracing your freedom is a clear, unwavering decision. There was a moment when I had to look myself in the mirror and say, "Enough is enough."

That decision to quit, to truly commit to freedom, was the **starting point** of everything. It wasn't just about quitting in the moment—it was about deciding to take full ownership of my future.

So, ask yourself right now: "Am I really ready to say goodbye to porn? Am I willing to commit to this journey, no matter how hard it may get?" This commitment must be clear and resolute.

Action Step: Write down your commitment. Look at it every day. Make it your mantra: *I am free from porn. I choose a healthier, better life.*

2. Remove Triggers and Temptations

For me, this was one of the most crucial steps. If I was surrounded by temptations—easy access to porn, old habits, and reminders—it was almost impossible to stay clean. It was like trying to swim upstream in a current.

Practical Actions:

- **Delete all apps and subscriptions** that make it easy to access porn. This might seem obvious, but it's critical. Remove the tools that allow you to fall back into old habits.
- **Install filters and blockers** on your devices. This is not about doubting yourself; it's about **creating a barrier** to stop your impulses before they happen.
- **Rearrange your environment**: If certain areas of your house or certain activities trigger you (for example, being alone in your room late at night), change your routine. Go to new places, spend more time in public areas, and create physical boundaries that make it harder for you to relapse

3. Build New Habits to Replace Old Ones

Porn is an addiction, and addiction thrives on **habits**. To truly break free, you must replace the old, harmful habits with new, healthy ones. This was a huge game-changer for me.

When I quit, I had to **retrain my brain** to crave something other than porn.

Action Step:

- **Exercise Regularly**: I found that physical activity helped me channel the energy I used to waste on porn into something positive. It boosted my mood, reduced stress, and gave me the physical and emotional strength I needed to keep fighting.
- **Develop a Morning Routine**: Having a solid morning routine was a key habit for me. This could include meditation, journaling, prayer, or even something simple like making a healthy breakfast. The more I focused on **starting my day right,** the less likely I was to give in to old habits.
- **Replace Mindless Time with New Hobbies**: If you've spent years watching porn during your free time, you'll need to find new ways to fill that void. I began reading, picking up a musical instrument, and taking up hobbies I'd neglected in the past. These things became part of my new identity and helped me embrace the future.

4. Emotional Regulation: Learning to Manage Your Feelings

One of the biggest challenges I faced in quitting was learning how to deal with the emotions that led me to porn in the first place. For me, it was often stress, loneliness, or boredom. I needed to learn how to handle these emotions without turning to my old coping mechanism.

Action Step:

- **Practice Mindfulness**: Mindfulness was a powerful tool in my healing process. Taking a few minutes every day to simply sit, breathe, and focus on the present helped me disconnect from the emotional triggers that would send me spiralling toward porn. **Mindfulness apps** or even free YouTube videos can guide you if you're just starting.
- **Journal Your Feelings**: Journaling became a way to **release** the emotions I was feeling without resorting to old behaviors. It allowed me to look at my emotions objectively and process them in a healthy way.
- **Seek Therapy or Counseling**: If you're struggling with deep emotional wounds, consider speaking to a professional. Therapy helped me uncover the emotional triggers and patterns I hadn't even realized were there.

5. Create a Support System

This journey doesn't have to be a solitary one. One of the biggest factors in my success was learning to **lean on others**. Having a support system in place gives you someone to talk to, someone to hold you accountable, and someone to remind you that you're not alone.

Action Step:

- **Find an Accountability Partner**: This could be a friend, mentor, or even a therapist. I had a close friend who knew about my struggle, and we held each other accountable. Being able to call someone when I was feeling weak helped me stay on track.
- **Join a Support Group**: If you're more comfortable with a group setting, consider joining a support group. There are online forums,

in-person groups, or even apps designed to support those quitting porn.

- **Talk to Your Partner**: If you're in a relationship, being honest about your struggles and involving your partner in your recovery can strengthen your relationship. It might feel difficult at first, but I can assure you that openness breeds trust and understanding.

6. Focus on Your Personal Growth and Self-Improvement

I learned early on that quitting porn wasn't the end—it was the **beginning** of a new chapter. This chapter was about growth. Every step I took to improve myself made it easier to stay free from addiction.

Action Step:

- **Set Personal Goals**: This can range from getting in better shape, advancing in your career, learning a new skill, or improving your relationships. Keep your goals front and center—they give you something to strive for and keep your mind focused on the future, not the past.
- **Embrace Discipline**: Building discipline in other areas of your life makes it easier to stay disciplined in your recovery. The more disciplined I became in my fitness, career, and daily routines, the easier it was to resist the pull of porn.

7. Be Patient and Compassionate with Yourself

Let's be clear: the journey to freedom from porn will not be perfect. There will be setbacks. There will be days when you feel weak or discouraged. But remember this: **you are human**, and recovery is a process, not a destination.

I learned to forgive myself for any slip-ups, but I also recommitted every single time. It was the consistency, not perfection, that led me to lasting freedom.

Action Step:

- **Practice Self-Compassion**: When I made mistakes, I was hard on myself. But I quickly learned that self-pity only made things worse. Instead, I practiced self-compassion. I would remind myself that I was doing the best I could, and each day I chose to get back up was a victory.

Conclusion: Your Freedom Starts Now

The journey from addiction to freedom is long and difficult, but it is also **possible**. It's not about quitting once—it's about committing to a lifetime of freedom. Every day, with every decision, you are building a life that is free from the chains of porn.

Take these steps, trust the process, and keep moving forward. The freedom you want is closer than you think. Believe in yourself, and embrace the incredible potential of the life that lies ahead.

You've got this.

Conclusion – A New Beginning

As I look back on my journey to quit porn and masturbation, I can't help but feel an overwhelming sense of gratitude. The road wasn't easy, and at times, it felt impossible. There were moments when I didn't believe I could break free from the chains that had held me for so long. But through every struggle, every setback, and every victory, I learned something valuable.

The first step was acknowledging the darkness I was living in—the isolation, the shame, the brokenness. I had to face the truth about how porn was affecting my life, my relationships, and my sense of self-worth. Once I recognized that truth, I could no longer ignore the pain and damage it caused. I had to make a choice: to keep going down the same path or to take control and reclaim my life.

It wasn't an instant transformation, but over time, I began to see change. I learned to manage my urges, to replace unhealthy habits with healthier ones, and to build a support system that kept me accountable. I learned the importance of self-care, emotional regulation, and setting new goals. And most importantly, I realized that my freedom wasn't just about quitting porn—it was about **embracing the life I was meant to live**.

Now, I'm living proof that it's possible to break free from the grip of addiction. My relationships are stronger, my self-esteem is restored, and I have a sense of purpose that I never thought I would find again. I'm no longer controlled by the shame and guilt that once defined me. I've learned to love myself, to honor my boundaries, and to pursue the future I've always dreamed of.

If you're reading this and you feel stuck in the same cycle, I want you to know that you **can** break free. It won't be easy, and it won't happen overnight, but with every small step forward, you are moving closer to the life you deserve. The darkness doesn't have to define you. You are capable of more, and you have the strength to reclaim your life.

Your journey won't be without challenges, but know this: you are not alone. There's a community of people who have been where you are and who are ready to walk with you every step of the way. You are worthy of the life that lies beyond the addiction. And I believe, just as I did, that you can overcome it.

This is the beginning of something beautiful. A new chapter. A new life. You have the power to make it happen. It starts now.

References

1. Carnes, P. (2001). *Out of the Shadows: Understanding Sexual Addiction.* Hazelden Publishing.
   - o This book is a foundational resource on understanding sexual addiction, including porn addiction, and provides insight into the psychological and emotional impacts it can have on individual

2. Cooper, A., & Griffiths, M. D. (2016). *Sexual Addiction: A Global Perspective.* Routledge.
   - o This book provides an in-depth analysis of sexual addiction from various psychological and cultural perspectives, offering helpful frameworks for understanding and overcoming addiction

3. Laaser, M. (2004). *Healing the Wounds of Sexual Addiction.* Regal.
   - o Laaser's book is a guide for those struggling with sexual addiction, focusing on healing emotional wounds, rebuilding relationships, and finding long-term recovery.

4. Greenfield, D. N. (2017). *Virtual Addiction: Sometimes New Technology Can Create New Problems.* New Harbinger Publications.
   - o This book explores how technology, including pornography, has impacted individuals' mental and emotional well-being, and offers strategies for breaking free from addiction.

5. Kroska, E. (2019). *The Pornography Addiction Workbook: A Guide to Overcoming Compulsive Sexual Behavior.* New Harbinger Publications.
   - o This practical workbook provides actionable steps for those seeking to quit pornography, featuring strategies for habit replacement, emotional regulation, and rebuilding self-worth.

6. West, L. (2018). *The Porn Trap: The Essential Guide to Overcoming Pornography Addiction.* Health Communications, Inc.
   - A comprehensive guide addressing how pornography addiction affects the brain, relationships, and personal life, along with actionable steps to reclaim one's life.